MODERN DAY PARENTING

How to Parent a Teen from a Teen Perspective

TENNY COLEMAN

DEDICATION

This Book Is Dedicated To All Parents

TABLE OF CONTENT

INTRODUCTION

Teen years are some of the most turbulent between a parent and a child. Often, you want to impart wisdom to them, but they don't want to hear what you have to say. After all, you "don't know what it's like to be a teen today". Wouldn't you love to have a book that could help bridge the communication gap?

I'll show you how to be the parent your teenager requires without fighting, frustration, or fear of getting it wrong. And to do that, you must know and truly understand their world, so you can collaborate with them.

I'm guessing that for many of you, this isn't the first time you've searched for advice on how to be a better parent. And since you're here, I'm guessing you're still not sure whether you've found what you're looking for. There is so much information and advice out there that it can be overwhelming.

I wrote this book for two reasons:

First, for you to be an effective parent, guide your child through adolescence, be fully informed, more woke than any other generation of parents and to understand how teenagers thinks.

The second reason is to provide you with hope. So if you have been concerned or afraid that you don't just have what it takes to be the parent your child needs you to be, I want you to put those fears to rest.

Do you have a teenager or a twenty-something that you are responsible for parenting, coaching or leading? You need to read this book. Do you know a teenager or twenty-something in your family, neighborhood, your church, community, or kids of friends? Then this may be a very viable book to pass on to their parents/guidance.

CHAPTER ONE

A JOURNEY INTO TEENAGERS LIFE

The life of a teenager seems to change daily.

In some ways, being a teenager is the most difficult stage of a teen's life. This is the stage where they are trying to define themselves not only to those around them, but also to themselves. One minute, a teen seems interested in a new sport, topic in school, or type of music, only to completely shift gears the next. Teenagers work to develop their personalities and interests during this time of great change, as they are constantly exposed to new ideas, social situations, and people.

Before their teenage years, these adolescents focused on school, play, and gaining approval from their parents. But now, those former goals are replaced with a desire for independence as teenagers work toward becoming young adults. Teenagers grow emotionally, cognitively, and physically during adolescence. These changes are not without difficulties, and this is where we really need our parents, even if we don't show it.

Everyone must go through the teenage years. Some of you have already passed this stage, others are on their way, and still others fantasize about the day when they will finally grow up! Teenagers today are very different from teenagers in the past. Everything about a teenager is distinctive, from head to toe. They dress differently, they behave differently, and even their spoken language differs.

Teenagers are known for their moodiness, insecurity, argumentativeness, impulsiveness, impressionability, recklessness, and rebellion. Teenagers today are "a technology generation". For in today's world, cell phones, the internet, music, movies, and television are very important. An aspect worth mentioning is communication.

Teens' social lives have become increasingly reliant on Facebook,

WhatsApp, Instagram, TikTok, and Twitter. Their days aren't complete unless they have access to these social networks. Teenagers nowadays prefer to make friends online rather than in person.

Do you know that teenagers nowadays succumb to various influences? Friends are one of the influences. Teenagers prefer to hang out with friends most of the time rather than staying home. They gather around food stands on weekend, mostly to discuss the happenings of the previous week. They even go out with their friends at night.

Teenagers are particularly fond of fantasizing about becoming celebrities or influential figures. There is no doubt that the presence of multimedia encourages teens to enter the entertainment industry, even if their potential or talents have not been elevated to the standards of acting and singing.

Some modern youths lack moral principles and self-discipline. Majority of youths back then learned respect, courtesy, honesty, and righteousness at a young age and had enough self-discipline to uphold these values. However, these moral values and self-discipline are gradually fading over time, as most of the younger generations are gradually disregarding these ethics.

This is probably brought on by parents' lack of attention and excessive media exposure. It can be said that teenagers use social media for entertainment for more than 38 hours each week. Parents who are preoccupied at work are unaware of this issue. As a result, these teens learn a variety of things from the media, such as violence and bad behavior, which undermines their moral values and self-discipline.

Alcohol abuse is one of the most serious drug problems among teenagers who attend high school or college. One of the biggest problems affecting practically all communities, families, and schools is teen alcoholism. Teenagers start using drugs as a result of their extreme stress. Alcohol makes teenagers feel good and happy because it distracts them from their problems. As a result, they drink to escape reality or cope with stress, which can be very harsh for some teenagers.

Teenagers can be disobedient to their parents. They frequently act quite harshly toward their parents, disobey them, and ignore their counsel. The lack of communication between parents and teenagers is the main cause for concern. The parents may be preoccupied with their demanding careers or jobs and other commitments. It's possible that they don't fully understand what their child is doing when they are not present. Teenagers debate with their friends about a variety of issues. When they compare themselves to their peers, they may believe that their parents are not giving them enough freedom.

They are also influenced by popular culture, fashion, and music. For example, rock stars, music, and heavy metal influence teens to follow trends and dress differently. They wear all black makeup, which even parents dislike. As a result, parents began to ground their children, which made matters worse for them, and they became more rebellious toward their parents.

Most of us appear and act perfectly normal, but everyone is going through something. Everyone has heard the story of a really smart kid who appeared to be happy, but "all of a sudden" decided to commit suicide. Suicidal decisions do not come all of a sudden; rather, they develop gradually over time. Anyone who thinks the individual who killed themselves is merely evading responsibility is gravely misguided. This person had to go through weeks, months, or even years of internal pain, to finally make a decision to simply quit living.

I have trouble sleeping at times because I feel empty. The best way to explain this feeling is like you haven't eaten in two days, but instead of that pain being in your stomach, that pain is in your heart, and you can't just eat to feel full.

There are some major issues that I simply do not care about. I'm not sure what it is about being a teenager, maybe it's the raging hormones or the preprogrammed desire to displease our parents that seems to be in all of us that makes us want to do outrageous unnecessary things just for the sake of doing them.

It seems like everyone is having sex these days, which has made it a major concern for teens to put pressure on themselves about. Everyone treats you differently and silently judges you if you've had sex, but if you haven't, you're a loser. High school is all about silent judging. Everyone wants to make and keep as many friends as they can, so they will never express their true feelings to you. My best friend claims to love me in front of me, but I have no way of knowing how she really feels. She might not even like me at all. Those are the thoughts that the majority of teenagers have, and they are the thoughts that harm us. We are all convinced that everyone despises us and that we are completely alone. These things could very well be true, but it is better not to think about them and instead focus on loving yourself.

Most of us teenagers don't even know what gender we prefer to be with, although none of us will admit it. It still amazes me that people can still be scared to admit that we have 100% no idea what our sexual orientation is. There are also the homophobic people in schools that make it hard to be open about who you are.

Being a teenager is hard! Being a teenager is so difficult that many of us wish we could just skip this chapter and have everything figured out. The truth is, however, you can't skip around. You have to go through this part. For a short period of our adolescence, we must try to make this an exciting, enjoyable, and memorable time in our lives. Being teenagers, we are in that fortunate stage where everything is positioned to go our way.

We are young, energetic, feeling free and independent minded. I believe though that in this stage, we really need the guidance and support of our parents and older people.

Come with me to the next chapter where I will be discussing what a teen of today is actually experiencing. Let's go!

CHAPTER TWO
WHAT A TEEN IS ACTUALLY EXPERIENCING

As parents, you must first comprehend what your teen child is going through in order to parent him or her effectively. Yes, you were once teenagers as parents, but in a different generation. In order to know how to parent today's teens, you must comprehend how they differ from previous generations. Let's look at what teenagers in today's world are going through!

Many people believe that being a teenager entails going to school, having hobbies, and hanging out with friends. This is true; we do many things to entertain ourselves, but teenagers face many challenges, such as making good decisions, choosing the right environment and people, expressing emotions, and so on.

Today, it is easy to label the current generation of teenagers as oversensitive, entitled, and spoiled. Though, to some extent, this criticism is correct, if you look closely, you will notice that they have challenges that could be difficult for anyone. They live in an entirely different world than a few decades ago.

Teenagers today face a variety of challenges for a variety of reasons, and our parents must be aware of these challenges in order to parent us effectively. Let's have a look at a couple of them.

1. Nonstop Exposure

Thanks to the internet, no generation has ever been more informed than this one. There is a never-ending flow of knowledge and information in the online world. Although teenagers can choose not to utilize it, that would be like telling them to stay in a room during high school. This is implausible.

They go to the internet world and see everything, whether positive or negative, displayed. Unfortunately, negative aspects can have a negative impact on their mindset. When a teen is at home, he or she is in a safe place. Yet, they are not safe in the presence of advanced technology and are subjected to cyberbullying. They are exposed to pornography and violence at such a young age without knowing what they are doing. Typically, teenage boys develop a taste for pornography. As a result, even though adulthood is still several years away, childhood's innocence is cut short.

2. Bullying

Not only is cyberbullying prevalent, but so is bullying among peers. Bullying can occur at any age and in any setting. Nonetheless, it is intense during the school years. It could become extremely traumatic. Only a few people have escaped bullying in recent years.

A teenager is under pressure from family and friends to conform to certain standards and hobbies or face repercussions. Teenage life is like a minefield, full of nasty bombs that can be dangerous if stepped on. Furthermore, social media bullying is unavoidable in this context. As a result, it is extremely difficult for young people to avoid bullying on any platform.

3. Hormonal influences and puberty

A teenager faces a lot of pressures in his or her life, and his or her body trolls him as well. For no apparent reason, he is angry one moment and tearful the next. A teenager is not awkward by choice, but these mood swings are a natural part of their maturation.

And as your emotions ride the rollercoaster, you start sprouting pus-filled blimps on your face, gaining and shedding puppy fat from nowhere, growing hair in odd places, smelling quite pungent from your armpits and other less savory places, and half of you start bleeding on a monthly basis. What a blast.

4. Love

A teenager's first love is excruciatingly painful. The stirring feelings towards a girl or a boy are like a harsh journey. Nothing matters more in love than the decision to launch one's heart at someone. Loving someone takes over their life, and they think they will never be able to love someone intensely again. When the first relationship breaks up, they want to give up on everything in life, and many times, girls and boys commit suicide.

5. Independence and privacy

Teenagers are advised to act maturely, but they are frequently treated as children.

They struggle with a lack of privacy while desperately seeking independence.

6. Unhealthy and unrealistic expectations

Unhealthy expectations, such as the fear of failing exams, not being accepted into a desirable university, having a bleak future, having no money, and having no value in society, can result in terrible sleepless nights. All of this contributes to depression and anxiety.

The popular message from teachers and parents is: pass your GCSEs and get into university, or your life is over. At the end of the day, it's not the end of the world if you don't get the desired results.

7. Proms

Choosing that dress, getting a date, the dreadful sight of a spot on your chin being invited to a post-party. Weren't these supposed to be enjoyable?

8. Identity

Teenagers find themselves categorized into certain subgroups based on what they like and wear, ranging from geeks and goths to skaters and hipsters, and many struggle with the culture of having to fit in. What if you enjoy both black clothing and One Direction? Being pigeonholed can be soul-destroying.

9. Being painted in a similar light.

Due to a small percentage of so-called "hoodies" getting into trouble, teenagers have a terrible reputation. Yes, some teenagers are brats who treat adults badly. Similar to how some adults are violent criminals. On the other hand, many teenagers are decent, hardworking people who are becoming tired of being treated like they are all the same.

It would be beneficial for teenagers' futures if their parents did not place unnecessary pressure on them, as this could have a negative impact on their children. They undoubtedly face numerous challenges. Teenagers, who are already stressed, should not be treated harshly or strictly. To understand their feelings and concerns, family members, teachers, and friends should speak to them in a friendly manner.

Teenagers, on the other hand, should be aware of what is right and wrong because the decisions they make in life will either make or break their lives.

CHAPTER THREE
MODERN PARENTING MISTAKES

Teenagers are a perplexing and, at times, frightening part of nature!

But now I'd like to take you on a journey inside the minds of teenagers. To separate fact from fiction for you. Why? Because I see a lot of parenting advice about how to deal with teenagers. However, the advice given is from people who were teenagers in a different generation. Often, the tactics will exaggerate even minor issues, straining the relationship between the parent and the teenager.

So, in this chapter, I'm going to explain some common parenting mistakes, not to criticize your parenting, but to help you avoid the strained parental relationships I've seen all too often. Let's get started;

1. Privacy

If you don't have a reason, don't go through your child's belongings at random. You should not read your child's journal. This only undermines their trust and teaches them to be more deceptive. Don't constantly inquire about your child's drinking or drug use. Believe them when they say they were somewhere.

I'm going to reveal one of the most closely guarded teenage secrets. ***"Their cellphones".***

One of the most harmful parenting techniques I've seen here is when parents go through their child's phone. Reading every text, conducting every internet search, and scrutinizing every social media platform, I cannot emphasize how dangerous and humiliating this is!

You might believe that by doing this, you are being a good and responsible parent, but all you are really doing is creating the deceptive teenager you were trying to prevent.

Talking about deceptiveness, one faithful evening, I was showing my younger brother and sister a fun picture on my phone when my mum walked into the living room and meet us laughing. She asked why we were laughing, and I showed her the picture. She took the phone from me to see it clearly, and she laughed as well. But instead of returning the phone, she began to flip through my pictures, and I didn't even know what she was doing. She soon saw a picture of me and a female friend of mine sitting on my laps. She was very mad at me because of that. She even reported me to my dad, and they both scolded me.

Scolding me didn't stop me from snapping more pictures with girls in even more compromised positions. Rather, it only taught me to be smarter and never allow my parents to see my phone, and I became smart at hiding some pictures and other odd things on my phone. I also became afraid of talking to my parents about relationships with the opposite sex, and until this day I don't talk about relationship matters with them, and my siblings don't either.

In this modern era, our phones have become an integral part of our lives. It is an essential organ for a teen, but this time it is located outside the body and requires charging. On there, we store a lot of our lives. Whether it's the problems we discuss with our friends, the query we Google because we were inquisitive, or the pictures we snap. To cut to the chase, phone is essentially a mini version of ourselves.

It hurts to have someone essentially probe through your innermost fantasies, desires, and concerns. Sometimes we get curious, sometimes we want to share a problem with our pals, and sometimes we would like to watch hilarious cat videos at three in the morning.

We are independent individuals with our own thoughts and feelings. Just because we are related to you genetically, does not mean you have unrestricted access to every aspect of our lives. You lose all of our trust in you the moment you start looking through our phones. We start to hide what we do out of concern about criticism. We no longer consider you to be someone we can turn to for help. By doing this, we cut you off, take extraordinary precautions to maintain our secrecy, and occasionally get ourselves into sticky positions. All these because we felt betrayed.

I understand how strong the desire to 'protect' your teen is. But know that 99% of us will be fine; we will learn to cope in our own unique way. You simply need to be the person we can turn to when we are unsure how to handle a situation.

You should not be going through our phones and personal lives unless we have given you a compelling reason to be concerned.

2. Sex, Drugs, and Rock and Roll

Before we start, let's clarify a few things. I'm not going to suggest that you let your teen use drugs, consume alcohol, or engage in as much sex as they choose. To put it bluntly, this is a foolish statement.

Concerns here are frequently motivated by a desire to protect, similar to the previous theme. A desire which has been a very useful and vital part of parenting. However, I kindly request that you have an open mind and seriously consider your viewpoint on this part.

The truth is, whether you want them to or not, most teenagers will drink and have sex!

As difficult as it may be to accept the aforementioned, it is absolutely true. If there is a desire, we will find a method to get there.

One mistake many parents make is believing that something won't happen if their children aren't exposed to it or don't know about it. But in my experience, this is a far cry from reality. A lack of exposure frequently results in excessive and incorrect use of substances like alcohol or drugs.

"Knowledge is power. Information is empowering. Education is the foundation of progress in every society and family." I believe the above quote is extremely relevant. Rather than outright prohibiting alcohol, drugs, and sexual activities, teach your children about the potentially negative consequences of improper consumption.

Jack shared a story during a teenage discussion in church. He said his mother brought 3 condoms and a bottle of beer and placed them on the table in front of him and his older brother. She asked them to pick anyone or both items. His older brother didn't pick any, but Francis took the condoms. But after his mum finished explaining the uses and effects of both items, Francis quietly dropped the condoms.

Jack's story got me thinking all day after hearing it. I wished I heard someone who would explain to me what sex was all about, and I knew definitely that my parents were a no-go area, so I decided to ask my friends and classmates in school if they had ever had sex or alcohol talks with their parents, but to my greatest surprise, only 3 out of 50 friends and classmates said yes.

Conversations must take place, regardless of how awkward they may be. I've seen friends use alcohol to numb their pain, drugs to forget about the world, and sex to make them feel valuable. Unfortunately, they all had parents who neglected to explain these ideas to them. They were merely instructed to refrain from doing it.

Explain consent and safe sex techniques to your teen. Tell them you'd prefer they wait if you want to. However, don’t make them feel like a criminal for their very natural desires. Explain responsible drinking; why alcohol shouldn't be used as a numbing agent, and the negative effects of abusing alcohol constantly. In other words, give them the power to understand the decisions they are making and the consequences of their choices.

4. Equal treatment

When I was in grade 7, my dad's friend was transferred to another town. He asked my dad to allow his daughter to stay with us so that she could complete grade 9, which he accepted.

During her stay, my dad showed preferential treatment to her over us, his biological kids. Her needs are met with immediate effect, while ours have to wait for 3 or more days. We are flogged and punished whenever we mess up, but she is not. The worst punishment my dad ever gave her was word of mouth. We hated our dad during that period of time because of his partial way of treating us. But I thank God that this unfair treatment stopped when the girl in question left our house. So you can imagine the damage this would have caused if the girl had stayed with us for a longer period.

It isn't fair to allow your son to stay out until midnight at age 16, but make your daughter come home at 9 pm. Make sure to enlist the assistance of both your son(s) and daughter(s) in tasks such as cleaning the house, doing dishes, mowing the lawn, taking out the trash, and assisting with grocery shopping.

I know, as humans, we can't control who we love, and as parents, we may love a child more than others, but don't make it obvious because it will cause a serious crisis in your family.

5. Negative Comparisons.

Teenagers often already have extremely low self-esteem. Consciously and unconsciously, we compare ourselves to our peers all the time. Take it from someone who has battled it for a long time. Even if we might occasionally respond negatively and speak ill of you, please understand that we are 100 times harder on ourselves.

It's all too easy to tell your teen; "X was just selected for the basketball squad!", "Y goes to the gym and goes for runs three days a week; you should go with him!", "Wow, did you notice how submissive all of your buddies are?"

While these may be said with no malicious intent, they can still have a greater impact than you may have previously imagined.

Consistently telling us about our peers' accomplishments can be misinterpreted by the teenage mind. We interpret your statement that we are not as good as the person you are referring to as an attack on us. Irrational? Yes. But this is the case. In reality, it stems from our own low self-esteem, from that little voice that tells us we're not as good as all of our friends.

But don't misunderstand what I've stated to mean that you can't order your teen to do anything or that they might wish to do XYZ. This is not true. Just be sure you strike a balance between letting us know what we are doing right and letting us know what others are doing or what you think we might like to do.

Additionally, avoid comparing our difficulties to those you faced as a teenager. Growing up was a challenging time for almost everyone. And the difficulties you faced may appear to be more difficult than those we faced. But that doesn't mean our emotions aren't real. Saying, "I had it much worse," invalidates what we are feeling.

Instead, try to empathize with your child. Even though it may seem like your teen is overreacting about not making the soccer team, or forgetting their homework, or being excluded, things like this feel like huge issues to teenagers.

6. EMOTIONS

Lucy narrates a personal experience on the day she first had her mood swing;

One day, after tennis practice, she felt like giving up on the sport. Her mother said they have committed to the team. The waves of emotions hit her so hard that she cried all the way home, but her mother was calm. She was expecting her mom to get mad at her, but she didn't. When she got home, she calmed down and realized she had her first mood swing.

From there, she got to learn about parenting. She advises, and I agree with her, that when a teen is experiencing a wave of emotions, the key for any parent is to stay calm. If the adult stays calm, the wave will pass and the teen will realize they were being silly. But if they fight back then, it may lead to an argument.

Being a teen is stressful, and sometimes we just need a break. Teenagers have a lot on their plate, including having to deal with the stress of getting good grades and high ACT or SAT scores, completing college applications, and participating in extracurricular activities.

Let them relax sometimes and don't constantly remind them to do this or that; sometimes they just need a break. Furthermore, if your child is no longer interested in a sport they are good at, let it go. You shouldn't force them to do a sport if they are not enjoying it.

CHAPTER FOUR
THE ULTIMATE NEEDS OF TEENS

While younger children require their parents to take the lead, teenagers require your support. When dealing with teenagers, we may employ many of the same techniques we used when they were younger. These include being encouraging and enabling, allowing children to learn from their mistakes rather than' showing them how to do it,' accepting that they may do things differently than you, acknowledging and respecting their choices, following the child's lead rather than jumping in with ideas, being present and spending time focused on your teenager.

In this chapter, I'm going to explain some ultimate needs of today's teenagers, even if they don't ask their parents about them verbally, but believe me, they do need them. Let's dive in;

1. Love and Concern

We all need to feel safe and protected, and our physical needs for food, clothing, warmth, and healthcare must be met. A conflict between parents' desire to meet these needs and a teenager's apparent desire to frustrate or be unrealistic about them may be one of the flash points with teenagers.

Teenagers could resist your efforts to keep them safe by staying out late, hanging out with “bad company,” and engaging in behavior that you might deem unsafe. They might disagree with you on every point. They might start abruptly to dislike tedious tasks like dental and health exams.

But just because they start acting differently doesn't mean they don't still want you to care about them and advocate for them. You talking about these topics and finding a middle ground with them would be beneficial. You can move forward when you are clear about your concerns and the outcomes you would want to see, but you are also open to hearing their point of view.

Teenagers want your love, care, respect, and attention just as much as they did when they were children. They want your attention. Too often, we ignore teenagers because they are moody and withdraw into themselves. Ignoring bad behavior and refusing to respond to it is one thing; ignoring the person who is bothering us is quite another. And it can develop into a pattern where they complain and we ignore them, so they complain even more, leading them to believe we don't care.

2. Family

Teenagers still have a desire to spend time with their parents. Yes, they want to be on their phones, playing games and communicating with their friends at all hours of the day and night. When given the chance, they want to spend time with them as well, whether it is out socializing or at each other's houses.

However, they still place high importance on spending time with family, whether it's eating together at the table, watching TV together as a family, or even going out as a family. That is why one fundamental aspect of family life that appears to have vanished may be something you need to defend or restore: the family meal.

Many families have discovered that sharing meals as a family has become a luxury they no longer have. One reason could be the fast pace of life; you and your children may have so many competing demands that it's difficult to find an hour each evening when you can all be together.

If you are under time constraints and choose meals that are simple to prepare, you may also be offering dishes that can be done individually, so there appears to be no reason why you should all be at the table at the same time. And, of course, if people's preferences and food fads have resulted in them eating different foods anyway, it may seem just as reasonable for them to get their own whenever they want.

Sharing family meals has the added benefit of making everyone at the table feel valued and appreciated, which is another essential need for teenagers.

3. Recognizing and respecting their decisions

Teenagehood is a time for choices. It's when they have to decide what courses they will study and what path they will take, at least for their early life. But they also have so many other decisions to make. Parents and teenagers can argue over so many of the options the young person decides upon.

Parents may say this is because the young person is making choices based on inexperience and on temporary and trivial deciders—choosing a college because friends are going there rather than because it's the best teaching environment for them, for instance.

Recognizing and respecting their choices doesn't mean you have to sit back and not give them some guidance. Acknowledging and respecting their choice means saying that you can see why they feel it is important, explaining your thoughts on the matter, and inviting them to tell you more in a mutually respectful way.

The end result could be a compromise or your both agreeing on one or the other course of action. You are more likely to achieve a satisfying and safe result if you begin by recognizing they have a point of view that deserves an audience.

4. Belonging

Allow teens privacy and some personal space. As kids move through the teen years, they spend more time with friends and less time with family. This is normal and okay. Teenagers need to socialize with their peers so they can begin to form their identity and broaden their social network. This does not mean that parents should just let go of their teenagers. This is a time when they need the support of parents more than ever. Think of it like flying a kite. It can only fly freely and safely when it is tethered to the holder.

5. Enjoyment

Let your teen make some decisions about how the family might spend a weekend or evening together. Play games together, laugh and have fun. Make the family and home a place of joy as much as possible. Encourage safe risk-taking in things like sports, public speaking, or getting involved in something new.

6. Power

Give your teen the opportunity to make some decisions. Keep firm rules for the things that have to do with safety or family values. Allow your child to make mistakes, and then talk to him/her without criticizing the outcomes and what they could do differently next time.

7. Teenagers require stimulation and activity, as well as rest and relaxation.

Teenagers today appear to be surrounded by an abundance of things to do and ways to learn. It's not uncommon for a teenager to arrive home late from school due to an after-school activity, then go straight to their phones and message friends while watching a show or playing online games with their friends.

Teenagers require activity as well, and not just 'activities' like meetings or clubs, but also physical exercise. During school breaks, kids tend to stay fit by running around. Teenagers frequently require assistance in staying active so that it becomes a part of their adult lifestyle, and they remain healthy and fit.

If they aren't participating in after-school sports, try to make exercise a family activity. This has the added benefit of giving you one more opportunity to spend time with them while running, cycling, swimming, or going to the gym.

8. Independence

Change your approach from telling your child what to do to asking for his or her input on how something like a chore will be completed. Most parents find this difficult because they believe they are losing control of their child. Allow your child to skip some family activities in order to spend time with friends. However, make sure to let him/her know what you expect of them, including any restrictions on using drugs or alcohol or late-night hours. Parental responsibilities start to change during adolescence from “life manager” to “life advisor.”

Teenagers, like all other humans, have needs. They are driven to become their own people as emerging adults. Parents all agree that they want their children to grow up to be responsible adults. By helping them meet these basic but strong needs, parents can facilitate growth and move their teens down a path to success.

CHAPTER FIVE
HOW TO BUILD A STRONG RELATIONSHIP WITH YOUR TEEN

As any parent knows—or has been warned—a child's adolescent years can be the most difficult. It can be especially difficult if their parents are divorced or separated.

Any parent may find it difficult to deal with the fast-paced effects of puberty, hormones, high school, and the rising yearning for independence. Every day can feel like a battle in a household with a teenager, sometimes over trivial matters. As a parent, you want to be able to love and guide your child as you always have, but you must recognize that as they change, so must your relationship with them. These are formative years in their lives, and it's important for them to know that their parents are there for them and are willing to recognize that they have a young adult who deserves their respect and guidance.

As a parent, you've undoubtedly watched out for your child throughout their childhood. They crave independence and the freedom to make their own choices now that they are adolescents. As children grow into teenagers, they gain a great deal of independence. This is a normal and natural part of growing up. But, even as they gain independence, we must maintain the same closeness to them that we did when they were small children. They still require our love, guidance, and amusement.

Even if your teen wants to be in charge of their own lives, you as a parent need to exert some kind of control and authority. Although a teen may be convinced that they know everything there is to know and that they're old enough to make their own decisions, a lack of life experience can hinder them from making the right decisions. This ties into the fear of any parent: that their teen will begin moving toward harmful behaviors.

Teenagers frequently test their personal limits and experiences, and they might be particularly vulnerable to peer pressure. Even though you can't watch over your teen's behavior at all times, you can serve as a source of authority and someone they can confide in. Just make sure you're letting your kid know that you're there and that any worries you have are genuine and for their own good.

Communicating that you recognize your child's adolescent independence but that the parent is still in charge is critical for establishing healthy boundaries and building a strong family structure. The goal is to raise a healthy, well-balanced young adult who knows right from wrong, cares about others, and is confident in their own abilities. This may appear to be a difficult task, but the adolescent years are the best time to begin.

Here are five tips to keep your relationship with your teenager strong and happy for both of you:

1. Spend time with each other.

It suddenly becomes far less cool to hang out with parents when a youngster turns into a teen. However, enhancing family structure can encourage and boost a teen's sense of wellbeing, while also giving them a chance to confide in a parent. I would advise family meals (without the TV on or cell phones present), joint chores (washing of plates together with my mum was my favorite bonding activity), board game nights, or volunteering as good examples of bonding activities. Any way you can make your teen aware that you are present can be beneficial as they navigate adolescence.

2. Lead by example.

You don't have to be a saint, but teens should look up to their parents as role models for their own behavior. Be mindful of how much drugs and alcohol you consume in front of your teen, as they may quickly imitate what they see as acceptable habits at home.

3. Set boundaries.

You may have a young adult in the house, but you are still the primary caregiver, and you must ensure that your child understands that you are the one who sets the boundaries. The National Institute on Drug Abuse Trusted Source emphasizes the importance of setting boundaries for your teen in a calm and firm manner. Not providing boundaries can lead to teens going into adulthood with the disjointed sense of having too much freedom.

4. Be Respectful

Teenagers these days have more to worry about than ever when it comes to criticism and taunts because of the popularity of cyber-bullying. To a sensitive teen, taunting might feel like torment. No matter how subtly, avoid making fun of your teen and desist using insulting language. Teenagers' self-esteem may suffer after hearing this from a parent or other authority figure, and they may also feel uncomfortable and unsafe at home.

5. Show you care.

It's critical that your teen feels loved and supported by their parents during these trying times, whether it's by making them a special lunch or sending them notes. If you have a disagreement with your teen, apologize and emphasize that you love them no matter what. Focus on the family unit's strength and unconditional love, and encourage your teen to be a part of it as well.

It's not always easy to be a teen's parent, but it's well worth the effort to cultivate a strong, healthy relationship that promotes respect and love between both parties. Although every teenager is unique, it is critical that a parent provide both guidance and support as their child navigates the storm of adolescence.

IDEAS TO CONNECT WITH YOUR TEEN

I'd advise doing something your teen enjoys if you're looking for ideas on alternative ways to connect with them. You could ask him/her to explain what they're doing in the game if it's video games. Alternatively, you could try baking a favorite meal or a new recipe together. Does your teen enjoy being creative and/or doing crafts? If so, visit a fun pottery studio or enroll in a painting class. Change into some comfortable clothes, put on some music, and do a puzzle together—or plan a family game night. Is your child interested in going to the gym? If so, try signing up for a class together or asking them to train you.

Whatever the case may be, the point is to do something with them! Even if you're just sitting around watching TV, that counts as being together. After dinner, take a quick walk around your neighborhood or to a nearby park.

Sharon shared the following reasons for her strong bond with her mother:

My mom has gone out of her way throughout my childhood to connect with me. And she would even help her friends connect with their teens. She would do this by planning Mother/Daughter outings for the two of us, along with my friends and their moms. It was so fun for all of us to spend quality time together. We had mother/daughter book clubs once a month, mother/daughter tea parties, mother/daughter day trips to a local lake or park; and mother/daughter dinners (which we still do often). I think since my mom started this at such a young age, I've gotten really used to hanging out with her, along with a friend and their mom, and we all look forward to it!

For me, the best way I felt connected to my parents was during joint chores. I share most of my problems with my mom whenever we wash dishes together, while I connect more with my dad when we wash his car together.

JUST REMEMBER

It's important to remember that they, like everyone else, will want their alone time, so don't be offended if they don't want to hang out with you all the time. They still care about you! But make it clear that you are still present. And that you are willing to spend quality time with them whenever they are ready.

The teenage years are exciting times, and the experiences we have during this time shape who we will become. Both teens and parents require each other and are fortunate to have them during these exciting times.

LAST WORDS

I hope that reading this has provided you with some insight into the thoughts and world of your teenager. I hope it has become clear to you from the standpoint of the teenager why some parenting techniques are more detrimental than they are beneficial.

To put it simply, every kid is unique. Therefore, in the end, you must follow your instincts and raise your teen in the way you believe is best. But constantly keep in mind that even though they are your child, they are also their own unique being.

www.ingramcontent.com/pod-product-compliance
Lightning Source LLC
LaVergne TN
LVHW050336160826
845677LV00014B/3642

9798353420880